DEMCO

The Abominable Snowman

by
Barbara Antonopulos

A
cpi
Book

From

RAINTREE CHILDRENS BOOKS
Milwaukee • Toronto • Melbourne • London

18 19 20 21 22   89 88 87 86 85

Library of Congress Number: 77-21387

Cover illustration, Lynn Sweat
Illustrations on pages 7, 14, 28, and 34, Nilda Scherer
Photos on pages 8, 20, 31, 36, and 47, Wide World Photos
Photos on pages 18, 19, and 23, United Press International, Inc.
Photo on page 25, Terry Fincher/Woodfin Camp & Associates
Photo on page 40, Bruce Coleman, Inc.
Photo on page 41, Craig Aurness/Woodfin Camp & Associates
Neanderthal Restoration photo, page 43, The American Museum of Natural History
Photo of bear on page 43, Bruce Coleman, Inc.
Photo of gorilla on page 43, G. B. Schaller/Bruce Coleman, Inc.
Photo of monkey on page 43, Leonard Lee Rue IV/Bruce Coleman, Inc.
All photo research for ths book was provided by Roberta Guerette.
Every effort has been made to trace the ownership of all copyrighted material in this book and to obtain permission for its use.

Library of Congress Cataloging in Publication Data

Antonopulos, Barbara, 1947-
   The abominable snowman.
   SUMMARY: Briefly describes evidence that large ape-like creatures, or Yeti, live in the Himalaya Mountains.
   1. Yeti—Juvenile literature. [1. Yeti]   I. Title.
QL89.2.Y4A57   001.9′44   77—21387
ISBN 0-8172-1053-9 lib. bdg.

Manufactured in the United States of America
ISBN 0-8172-1053-9

Contents

Chapter

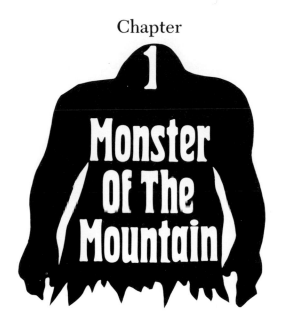

1
Monster Of The Mountain

A small group of men made their way slowly up the steep mountain slope. The air was still. No one spoke as they climbed. Each man thought only of the blinding white snow and the steep mountain still ahead of him.

Suddenly, the men froze in terror. Heading straight at them was an ugly, ape-like creature. Were they imagining it—or was the creature making an eerie, whistling sound?

Before they could answer that question, the beast attacked one of the men, knocking him down. The beast tore at his flesh. The others were frightened, but they rushed to help their friend. The ugly beast turned. Its glowing eyes glared at them.

Then, as suddenly as it had started, the creature stopped its fierce attack. Quickly, it turned, scrambled up the mountain slope, and disappeared among the rocks.

Was this the nightmare of snow-weary adventurers? No. The story was told by a group of respected Norwegian mountain climbers. They came upon the creature in the Zemu Pass in eastern Nepal.

These mountain climbers were not the first to describe the creature. For hundreds of years, stories of this "monster of the mountain" have been told. And for all these years the questions and answers have been the same. *What does it look like?* Eyes that glow . . . long matted hair . . . body larger than a human's. *Was it an ape? Was it a giant?* Who can tell? From the icy stillness of the highest mountains in the world, the creature stalks the Himalayan villages.

The beast glared at the men as they helped their friend.

Some stories describe the creature hunting animals by night. Others are tales of the terror it brings to humans—savage attacks and brutal killing. Who is this terrible creature that stalks the snow-covered Himalayas? We know it only as the *Abominable Snowman*.

Nepal is a small and very beautiful country in Asia. Wedged between India and Tibet, Nepal is the home of the most daring mountain-

The Himalaya Mountains challenge adventurers from all over
the world.

climbing area in the world—the towering Himalaya Mountains. And looming over Nepal's border is Mount Everest, the highest and most challenging peak of all. There, among the giant snowcapped Himalayan peaks, the legend of the Abominable Snowman was born.

Many of the stories about the Abominable Snowman come from a single group of mountain people in Nepal—the *Sherpas*. The tough Sherpas live in these high mountains all through the year. Though the air is thin—it doesn't have much oxygen—it doesn't bother the Sherpas. They've been breathing this air for all their lives. These expert climbers know the area better than anyone else. They know the animals that live there. And they know the Abominable Snowman!

The Sherpa word for the Abominable Snowman is *Yeti*. *Yeti* can mean "one that lives among the rocks," "magical one," or "one that eats everything." Put these meanings together and they seem to describe the Abominable Snowman.

Just what does the creature look like? Some say it is as tall as a human. Reports of its height vary from five to eight feet. Some have reported the Snowman is as tall as 15 feet! The creature's long arms dangle from its body, the hands reaching past its knees. All agree that the Snowman has no tail.

But eyewitnesses don't agree about the color of the creature's hair. Some say it is red. Others say it is gray, black, or white. The Snowman also has an unbearable odor. That is why it is called "abominable."

The creature's head is dome-shaped with a point at the top. Long hair hangs around its hairless face. Amazingly, the face looks almost human. But that's where the similarity ends. The creature's mouth is wide and it has large teeth.

Legend says to beware of the Snowman's eyes. Large and deeply sunken, they are frightening! They glow like red-hot coals. Some even believe if you look into the eyes of the Snowman, you will die!

Chapter

2

Just How Abominable Is The Snowman?

When the Abominable Snowman is angry or startled, it makes a frightening sound. It cries with a long, high-pitched whistling sound that can be heard for miles.

The Snowman is as much a part of the Sherpas' life as their mountain home. In fact, Sherpa children are warned to be good, or "the Snowman will come to get you!" Stories about the terrible beast are passed from generation to generation of Sherpas. Their stories are filled with violence, fear, and death. When will the

11

monster strike? Who will be its next victim?
What can stop it?

Sherpa mountain-climbing guides often
bring back reports of the Snowman. One time
two Sherpas on the way home to their village
were stopped dead in their tracks. There on the
path ahead of them was the creature. It was eat-
ing a mountain goat that it had just killed. But
it had not yet seen the men. Then, sensing they
were watching, the Snowman looked up.

The Abominable Snowman glared at the two
men. Its angry eyes glowed. It seemed to be de-
ciding whether to attack or retreat to the mountains. The creature gave a howl and then whis-
tled its familiar cry. The men then knew it was
the Abominable Snowman.

From surrounding mountain slopes the cry
seemed to be repeated again and again. Were
there more creatures behind the rocks, waiting
to pounce? What would *this* Snowman do to the
men? The men did not want to find out. They
were about to run when the Snowman, still
whistling its high-pitched warning, turned and
made its way back up the rocks.

The Sherpas say there is not just one but many types of Snowman. They describe three creatures. The largest Snowman looks like a bear. The second, a middle-sized one, is very fierce and mean. Finally, there is a small Snowman that looks like a *monkey*. All are called *Yeti* by the Sherpas, but each type also has a name of its own.

The bear-like Snowman is called the *Dzu-Teh*. It is six to eight feet tall. Sometimes the *Dzu-Teh* walks on all fours. This creature has very long claws and shaggy hair. Although mainly a plant-eater, the *Dzu-Teh* also has been known to kill and eat animals.

The *Mih-Teh* is the Sherpas' name for the middle-sized Snowman. *Mih-Teh* means "the ape that preys on man." It is as tall as an average human. And, like a person, it walks on two legs. It is said to be the meanest beast in the Himalayas. The teeth of the *Mih-Teh* are large and square. Some people claim to have seen this beast with 12-inch fangs. It has shaggy black or red hair and a pointed head. When people speak of the Abominable Snowman, the *Mih-Teh* is probably the type they mean.

Mih-Teh

Thelma

Dzu-Teh

14

The smallest Snowman, called the *Thelma*, is about the size of a 15-year-old human. It lives in the lower regions of the mountains.

Is the Abominable Snowman fact or fantasy? Why hasn't one been captured? Why has no one taken any good photographs of the beast? All that the scientists and "monster hunters" have are casts of the giant footprints the creature has left in the mountain snow.

Chapter

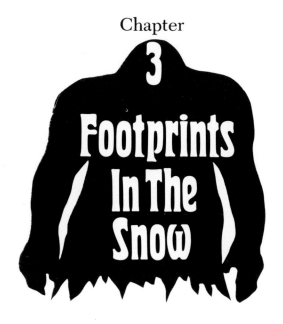

3

Footprints In The Snow

Footprints in the snow, believed to belong to the Abominable Snowman, have been found by Sherpas and other mountain climbers. Some people insist these footprints were not really made by an Abominable Snowman. They say the footprints were simply left by mountain bears or other animals prowling the snowy mountain slopes. But the tracks seem to be too large for ordinary animals.

Or perhaps when the sun softened the snow a little, the tracks melted together and became larger. Then the tracks would look as if they had been made by a huge beast. Another explanation is that snow or rocks falling from the mountains made the prints in the soft snow.

But the footprints looked so real that it was hard for some people to imagine that *anything* but an Abominable Snowman made them. If these are really the creature's footprints, they tell us much about the Snowman.

The Abominable Snowman's foot is somewhat different from a human foot. It is flat and has no arch. The big toe is very large. And it is widely separated from the rest of the foot. The second toe is long and thin. The remaining three toes are short and stubby.

The first reports of the Abominable Snowman reached the Western world during the 1880s. Since that time, people all over the world have been excited by the thought of such a monster. And they eagerly wait to hear more about the Snowman.

A few people have gone to the Himalayas to find out for themselves. Mountain-climber Eric Shipton was the first to photograph the Snowman's footprints in 1951. When he found the prints on a glacier in northeast Nepal, the world took notice. Perhaps there really was an Abominable Snowman!

The footprints Shipton photographed were large—12 inches long. The mountain climber

A large footprint was found on a Nepal glacier by mountain-climber Eric Shipton.

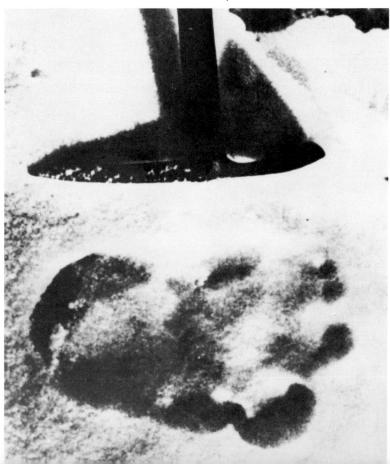

had never really believed the stories about the Abominable Snowman until he photographed its prints. Shipton knew that only a very large animal could have made these tracks. But where could he find an actual creature?

One of the men with Shipton was Edmund Hillary—a man whose name will always be linked to those high mountain peaks. When he returned from the expedition, Hillary was de-

Eric Shipton: until 1951, he didn't believe in the Abominable Snowman.

Sir Edmund Hillary, left, with his Sherpa guide, Tenzig Norgay.

termined to scale new heights in the Himalayas. He was also curious about the mysterious Snowman.

Two years later, on May 29, 1953, at 11:30 in the morning, Hillary and Tenzig Norgay, his Sherpa guide, made history in the Himalayas. They were the first men to reach the top of the highest mountain in the world, Mount Everest.

During their climb up Mount Everest, Hillary and Norgay had found what they believed were tracks of the Snowman. Now Hillary was even more curious about the strange creature. The first man to climb Mount Everest wanted another "first." This time Hillary wanted to be the first person to prove that the Snowman was real.

Chapter

4

Hillary's Search

Sir Edmund Hillary's expedition in the Himalayas in 1960 had two purposes. One was to learn how a person was able to breathe without much oxygen in the high reaches of the mountains. Secondly, Hillary wanted to learn how some creatures seemed to get along so well in the high mountains and thin air. *Hillary would hunt for the Abominable Snowman!*

Hillary wasn't out to shoot or kill a Snowman. But even if he had wanted to, the

Hillary became Sir Edmund Hillary when he was knighted by
Queen Elizabeth after he conquered Mt. Everest. By 1960 Hillary
set a new challenge for himself—he would find the
Abominable Snowman.

government of Nepal would not have permitted
it. It is forbidden to kill a Snowman. The
Snowman is an important part of the way of life

in Nepal. Besides, the religion of Nepal forbids the killing of all animals—even abominable ones!

Hillary only wanted to see the Snowman to take photographs of it. If there were a chance to trap one of the creatures, Hillary wanted to do so. But he wanted to trap it only long enough to study it. For that he would need only cameras, not rifles. Hillary set up cameras with wires in the snow. If a Snowman walked over a wire, the wire would snap the camera's shutter. The Snowman would have taken its own photograph.

Hillary brought other things to hunt the Snowman without harming it. He brought guns that fired harmless "bullets" filled with a drug that would knock out the Snowman. He also brought tear gas to protect the men in the expedition.

Hillary learned that the Abominable Snowman had been seen in the Rolwaling Valley, an area south of Mount Everest. Obviously, it was the best place for Hillary to begin his search.

During the expedition, Hillary lived in Beding, a small village in the valley. Beding had

A small village in the mountains of Nepal.

already had its share of visits from the Abominable Snowman. Living there, Hillary hoped to gather information about the creature from eyewitnesses.

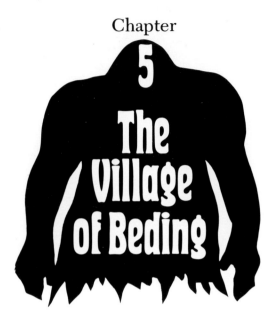

Chapter

5

The Village of Beding

The climb into Beding was long and difficult. The mountain peaks grew even steeper. And there were dangerous ledges and rocky cliffs. Hillary and his men were relieved when they finally made it.

They immediately set up camp and talked to the villagers who told some strange stories of the Abominable Snowman. One story was of particular interest to Hillary.

There had been one winter when the snow-fall was exceptionally heavy. It was the coldest and most bitter winter any of the villagers could remember. It was not the snow or bitter cold, however, that upset the villagers—it was the *Yeti*. Several had been seen lurking close to the village, and many people were frightened.

Throughout the winter, snow was piled deeply on the mountains around the village. Then one day the mountains above the village could no longer hold their heavy load. An icy white avalanche—tons and tons of snow—crashed down the slopes. The village was almost completely buried, and many villagers were killed. A strange quietness spread over the village after the roar of the avalanche stopped.

That night the quiet was broken by eerie cries that echoed through the village. High whistling sounds stabbed through the darkness. Who was making this horrible noise? The next morning the villagers found large footprints around the village. Were the *Yeti* also terrified of the avalanche? Were they seeking safety in the village? No one knows because no one had seen even one Snowman. And by morning the *Yeti* seemed to be gone.

The people of Beding had other tales to tell Hillary. One was about a monastery in Beding where the religious men, called *lamas*, lived.

One night as it began to snow the lamas were praying in their monastery. Suddenly, two of the *Yeti* approached the monastery. They walked slowly around the building. One even walked up and touched the building.

When they saw the *Yeti* at the window, the frightened lamas grabbed their cymbals and started to clang them.

Hearing noises, the lamas looked up from their prayers. There, at the window, were two horrible creatures—*Yeti*. And it looked as if they were about to climb through the window!

The lamas were scared. They quickly grabbed the cymbals they usually played in their prayer service. The lamas banged the instruments together and made as much noise as possible. Fortunately, the *Yeti* backed off, screeching their horrible cries as they ran. The lamas' quick thinking may have saved their lives.

Before they left the village of Beding, the head lama gave the Hillary team some advice about hunting the Snowman. He told Hillary that the clothes he and his men wore were too brightly colored. The Snowman could easily see them, and it would stay away. After a hurried change of clothes, Hillary set out on the next leg of the search—a trip to the famous Khumjung village.

Chapter

6

The Snowman's Scalp

The Hillary group moved slowly and carefully through the mountains. In every village along the way, their Sherpa guides would hunt for information on *Yeti*. *When had the Yeti been seen last?*

One of his Sherpa guides told Hillary that local villagers had watched *Yeti* retreating from his village into the Rolwaling Valley. Sure enough, within their first few days in the valley area, the

While trekking through the mountains, Hillary's team found the print of a bare foot in the snow.

Hillary team found footprints. They were the size of a large man's foot. But they were not the tracks of any ordinary man. They were of *bare feet*. And no man would go barefoot in the deep snow.

Hillary took photographs of the footprints and made plaster casts of them. Then he and his men continued their search. They were sure they were getting closer to the Snowman.

Hillary's party next made its way to a part of Nepal called Solu Khumbu. Many of the Sherpas traveling with Hillary were from this part of Nepal. They told Hillary that he would have better luck finding a Snowman there. According to the Sherpas, a monastery in the Solu Khumbu area had two scalps. They supposedly belonged to the *Yeti*. One scalp, the Sherpas said, was over 100 years old.

Hillary's mind bubbled with excitement. He couldn't wait to get to the monastery. *Could it be that these people actually owned the scalp of a Snowman?* With every step through the snow and over ice-covered rock, his excitement grew. He planned to convince the villagers to let him take the scalp out of Nepal for scientific study.

Hillary and his friends received a warm welcome from the Khumjung villagers. The Western guests were treated to a fine meal and dancing. But at first no one was offering to show Hillary the *Yeti* scalp. The Khumjung villagers were very superstitious. They believed that if the scalp were taken from them, it would anger the gods. Hillary tried to convince them otherwise. Talking gently to the older villagers, he tried to explain the scientific importance of his request.

After much discussion, Hillary was successful. The Khumjung villagers finally brought out the scalp. They first took turns trying it on. They even let Hillary put the large scalp on his head. It was a very funny sight. The scalp covered the top of Hillary's head, reaching down almost to his eyes. It was made of thick skin covered with black and red hair, and it was dome-shaped. But Hillary wanted more. He had to *prove* this was really the scalp of an Abominable Snowman.

Hillary wanted to have the scalp examined by scientists. Only then could he be sure that the scalp had actually come from the head of a Snowman. But such a study could only be done in a far-off city that had a large university, such as London or Paris.

In order to borrow the scalp for six weeks, Hillary had to agree to give money to the monastery at Khumjung. He also told the villagers that he planned to build a school for their children. Even though he had paid the villagers well, they were still doubtful about allowing the scalp to be taken.

The villagers finally agreed, but they demanded one more condition. Three of the Sherpas who were guiding Hillary had to stake

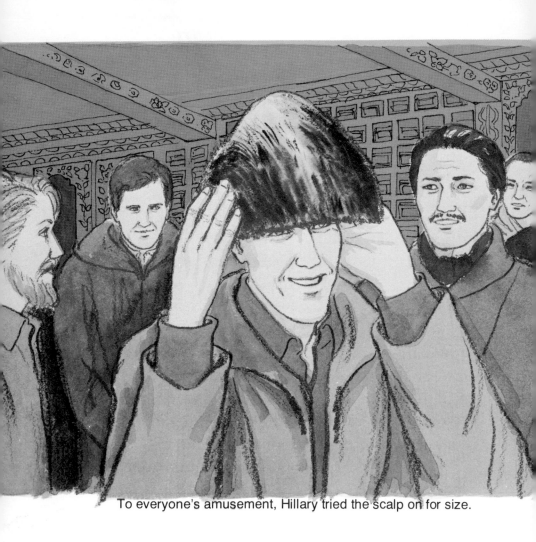

To everyone's amusement, Hillary tried the scalp on for size.

their village land on Hillary's honesty. If Hillary did not return with the scalp, these Sherpas would have to give their land and everything else they owned to the village.

Hillary wondered if his Sherpa guides would agree to this. They had already helped him so much. But the three men were willing to help Hillary again. Without asking any questions, they agreed to put up their land. The guides trusted Hillary, and they knew he would return with the scalp.

The scalp finally in hand, Hillary and his men made ready to leave for the United States. With them was a man from Khumjung, ordered to watch over the scalp of the Snowman. The villagers were still very superstitious. If the scalp were lost, the villagers feared it would anger the gods.

The scalp was examined by scientists in Chicago and Paris. But they didn't believe it had once belonged to a Snowman. In Chicago they believed that the "scalp" was really the hide of a *serow*—a wild goat antelope. The French experts said it was from a bear. The only thing both groups of scientists agreed on was that the scalp was very old. It had probably come from an animal that had died hundreds of years ago.

Perhaps the Khumjung scalp was not a Snowman's. But several questions were still unanswered. In the scalp were many *parasites*, tiny animals that feed off other living things. These parasites were not known to live off either serow or bears. The experts were puzzled.

Hillary returned to Nepal and gave the scalp back to the villagers. They were relieved to have their scalp back in Khumjung. And they refused to believe the scientists' reports. To them, the

The scalp, thought to be from an Abominable Snowman, was kept at a Himalayan monastery for about a century.

scalp *was* the Abominable Snowman's and no one could tell them otherwise!

Hillary was greatly disappointed. His experiences in Nepal had discouraged him from future *Yeti* expeditions. Poor Hillary! He had found footprints and scalps, but he had not seen one Snowman. His cameras had taken pictures of huge footprints, but not one photograph of the creatures. So there was still no proof. Perhaps no one could solve the mystery of the Abominable Snowman after all.

Chapter

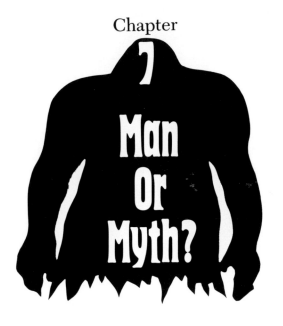

7

Man Or Myth?

Is the Abominable Snowman really an animal? Is it human? Or is it only a legend? Over the years, scientists, mountain climbers, and others have tried to puzzle out the mystery of this strange and frightening beast. But answers are not easy to come by. Some have concluded that there is no such thing as an Abominable Snowman. They think there are other explanations for the many sightings and stories of the horrible creature.

Certain experts believe that the *Dzu-Teh*, the largest Abominable Snowman, is actually the Tibetan blue bear. With its dark reddish-brown hair and dome-shaped head, this fierce animal could easily be mistaken for a Snowman.

But the Tibetan-blue-bear theory doesn't help explain the middle-sized Snowman. The fierce *Mih-Teh* usually walks upright, not on all four legs as bears usually do. Besides, the people who live in the Himalayas know the animals that live in their mountains. Surely they would be able to tell the difference between a bear and a monster!

It has also been said that the Abominable Snowman is actually a monkey. But the monkeys of the Himalayas are much smaller than all but the smallest Snowman, the *Thelma*. And when it comes to the larger, ape-like Snowman, there's no way it could be mistaken for a monkey.

Others say the Abominable Snowman is really a human being. Lamas, the religious men of Nepal, sometimes wander in the mountains by themselves. From a distance, dressed in their large hooded robes, they could be mistaken for a Snowman. But the Abominable Snowman is

A Malayan bear, relative of the rare Tibetan blue bear but found further south in East Asia. Could a bear have been mistaken for the Abominable Snowman?

fierce-looking. Lamas are not. Also, lamas could not possibly make the large, deep, barefoot prints that have been found in the Himalayan snow.

If the Snowman is not a bear, monkey, or man, what is it? Some people who have studied

Scientists agree that the scalp was very old—but was it from an Abominable Snowman, or could it have simply been the skin of a serow?

the Abominable Snowman believe the creature may be related to the *Gigantopithecus*, a prehistoric ape that lived in the Himalayas about nine million years ago. When prehistoric man moved into the Himalayas the apes were forced to go into hiding. The apes retreated from man and were rarely seen again. Perhaps over the years these prehistoric apes became *Yeti*. But again, there's very little proof for this idea.

In 1957, an American named Thomas Slick and two other men climbed the Himalayas. There they found footprints in three different places. Believing that the prints were made by a Snowman, they took photographs of the tracks.

Later, when the men came to one of the nearby villages, the people told them that two of the local children had recently sighted a Snowman. Slick asked the children to describe how the Snowman looked as it came toward them out of the woods. They said the Snowman was about seven or eight feet tall. Though they were terribly frightened, the Snowman did not harm them.

Slick showed the children several photographs—of a bear, a monkey, a prehistoric man,

When the children were asked to identify the creature they had
seen, they first pointed to an ape. Then, they chose the picture of
a prehistoric man!

and an ape. At first, the children pointed to the photograph of the ape as the one that looked most like the creature they had seen.

But then Slick took away the photograph of the ape. Again he asked the children which picture looked most like the Snowman. This time the children pointed to the picture of a prehistoric man!

Chapter

8

American Relatives?

Mysterious beasts like the *Yeti* are known by different names in other parts of the world. In many parts of South America, there have been reports of an Abominable Snowman that looks very much like the Himalayan beast. It, too, is big and fierce with long arms and a small head. Some witnesses have also said the creature has large green teeth!

The people of North America call their Abominable Snowman "Big Foot"—or the Indian name, "Sasquatch." Its tracks have been found in mountains and in forests. There are even some photographs of "Big Foot."

In 1967, two men camping in northern California supposedly spotted Big Foot. Luckily, they happened to have a movie camera along and were able to film the creature. However, because their film was often out of focus and quite blurred, it's hard to tell what these men really saw. The figure in the film was large and hairy. It is seen walking past the camera, pausing for a moment to look directly into the lens, and then retreating into the woods.

Some people think the film is a hoax. They say that the men created the tracks. They then dressed up as Big Foot to fool other people.

Like the Snowman in the Himalayas, Big Foot has not yet been proved to exist. But no one has proved that it doesn't exist. Because of the many footprints, pictures, and sightings, there is a chance the creature is real!

Stories of the Abominable Snowman and creatures like it may be frightening—but the

This large, hairy creature was photographed in 1967 in Northern California. Is it Big Foot?

mystery is fascinating. If these beasts are actually living in the mountains and forests around us, hopefully one day we will be able to prove that they do exist. By studying the Abominable Snowman, we may shed new light on the way people and animals have changed since prehistoric times. At this time, however, the strange case of the Abominable Snowman remains a *great, unsolved mystery.*